Welcomed *by* Name

Our Godchild's Baptism

Peg Bowman

LOYOLAPRESS.
A JESUIT MINISTRY
Chicago

LOYOLA PRESS.
A JESUIT MINISTRY

3441 N. Ashland Avenue
Chicago, Illinois 60657
(800) 621-1008
www.loyolapress.com

Acknowledgments for quoted material and photographs appear on page 18, which is to be considered
a continuation of the copyright page.

Cover and Interior Design: Judine O'Shea

ISBN-13: 978-0-8294-1800-2
ISBN-10: 0-8294-1800-8

Contents

A Christian Privilege   2

Why Baptism?   4

Sacraments: Signs That Are Real   6

Signs of Baptism: Welcoming and Anointing   8

Signs of Baptism: New Life in Christ   10

The Rite of Baptism: Before You Approach the Font   12

The Rite of Baptism: At the Font and After   14

Beyond Baptism: The Role of a Godparent   16

A Christian Privilege

Congratulations! You have been chosen to be a godparent.

Thank you! You have agreed to be a godparent. What a wonderful journey of faith you will share with this godchild and this family.

In the saving waters of Baptism, a baby will be bathed in grace and become a child of God. You have been chosen to participate in this first sacrament in a special way. This book has information and images to help you prepare for this Baptism and the life of grace that follows it.

What a joy it is to welcome a new baby by birth or by adoption! What an added joy to welcome a new child of God through Baptism! It is a blessing for the Church and for the world.

Every godparent is a sign of that blessing. You have been chosen because of some family or friendship bond. Your task, your ministry, is to be a role model for this child, a support in faith for this family, and a good example of one who lives the Christian life.

As you stand beside this child's parents on the day of Baptism, you will profess faith on behalf of your godchild and thus begin a lifelong relationship with a new member of the Church.

Although only one godparent is required, it is still quite common for those to be baptized to have both a godmother and a godfather. You are likely to be acting in concert with someone else to help with the godchild's spiritual and social formation in the coming years.

Write down your thoughts about being chosen as a godparent. What is your hope, what is your prayer, for your godchild?

Why Baptism?

Baptism marks the formal beginning of an infant's Christian life. Without Baptism there can be no sharing in the other sacraments. Baptism is "the gateway to life in the Spirit" (*Catechism of the Catholic Church,* 1213). No longer an "outsider," this child will be an "insider," a member of the Body of Christ, a person filled with God's own life.

During the Baptism liturgy, the priest or deacon will say to your godchild: "[Name], the Christian community welcomes you with great joy. In its name I claim you for Christ our Savior by the sign of his cross."

Being claimed for Christ is being claimed by God. God's grace is first. From all eternity God desires to share divine life with us. The Son of God became a human being to share God's life, God's grace, with us.

Like every human being born since our first parents (with the exception of Christ himself and Mary, the Mother of God), your godchild is born into the human condition. Sadly for everyone, sin is part of that condition. Original sin is part of human life. No one can avoid it.

But Jesus Christ has overcome sin and death. No one need be trapped forever in either. Jesus died and rose from the dead and ascended to the Father to free us from death and sin. In Baptism we become adopted children of God. In Baptism we receive salvation in Christ.

Sacraments
Signs That Are Real

How can we know anything about God or the life of a person? Probably the best way to know things is to experience them—seeing, touching, hearing, tasting. Experiencing things through the senses is part of being human. God communicates to us in these very human ways. Through the Church we have tangible, physical signs that not only tell us about God but also manifest God's presence to us. We call these special signs *sacraments*. They are God's mighty works.

Any sign points to something real, but sacraments do more than merely point. Sacraments *cause* what they signify. The Church's seven sacraments give us seven ways to experience God, to receive God's life, to meet God.

The Church itself is lovingly described as the sacrament of communion that brings us to Christ (*Catechism of the Catholic Church*, 1108).

Because the Son of God became a human being, all of human life can point to God. We can find something sacramental about many things in our everyday lives. Godparents help their godchild see and understand and appreciate this.

Signs of Baptism
Welcoming and Anointing

There will be much to notice at your godchild's Baptism. Each sign and symbol and each ritual action is important and has special meaning.

- **The gathered community** signifies the whole Church, standing to welcome this new member and assenting to the profession of our faith.

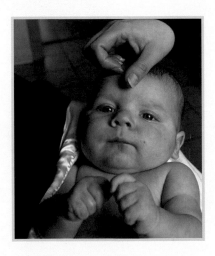

- **Signing with the cross** is one of the first ritual actions. The parents will be invited to join the celebrant in tracing the Sign of the Cross on their baby's forehead to claim this new member for Christ. Godparents, family members, and parishioners may be invited to do the same.

✧ **Anointing** occurs twice in the Baptism of small children. Before the immersion or pouring of water, the baby will be anointed on the breast with the oil of *catechumens*. This first anointing calls on Christ to strengthen the one who will be baptized. Later in the rite the baby will be anointed on the head with *chrism*. This second anointing—with sweet-smelling chrism, which takes its name from Christ—joins the newly baptized to Christ, who is Priest, Prophet, and King. Because of Christ, the newly baptized will be strengthened to live a life that is priestly, prophetic, and royal.

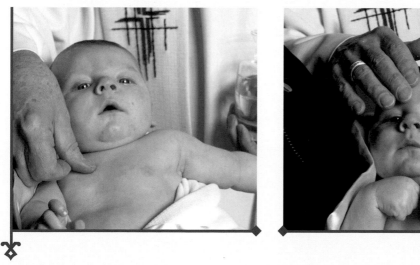 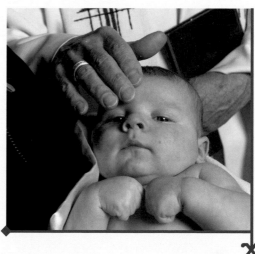

Signs of Baptism
New Life in Christ

Other signs of Baptism may be more familiar to you.

- **Water** is the central symbol of the sacrament of Baptism. The Church wants a generous use of water, whether the sacrament is by immersion, which is preferred, or by pouring. In this bath your godchild will be washed free from sin. In this bath your godchild will be buried with Christ but then raised up to new life in him. Even the prayer of blessing over the water will remind us of its power. Water can give life, save life, and take away life. In the waters of Baptism, sin is destroyed; new life emerges; all is clean, refreshed and new.

- **The baptismal garment** is provided by the family. It may be something new or something that has been used by the family for generations. It is usually white in color. This baptismal garment is an outward sign of your godchild's new life in Christ.

❖ **The lighted candle** signifies the light of Christ to be kept burning bright all through life. The Easter candle burns throughout the Baptism liturgy. You will light your godchild's own candle from this Easter candle.

How can you help your godchild keep this baptismal garment unstained and this light of Christ shining?

The Rite of Baptism
Before You Approach the Font

Whether your godchild is baptized during Sunday Mass or at another time on Sunday, the liturgy will follow the same basic outline. As godparent you will be an active participant in this celebration.

❖ The celebrant meets the baptismal party at the entrance to the church or baptistry and asks the parents, "What name do you give your child?" and "What do you ask of God's Church for your child?" Their answer is "Baptism" or "faith" or "the grace of Christ" or something similar. More questions will make sure that both parents and godparents understand their responsibilities. You agree to help the parents in their duty as Christian parents.

- The celebrant claims your godchild for Christ by tracing the Sign of the Cross on the baby's forehead and inviting first the parents and then you and others to do the same.

- The Liturgy of the Word is next. Biblical readings and the homily lead all those assembled to a deeper understanding of the mystery of Baptism.

- Intercessions with a short litany of the saints, which may include your godchild's patron saint, follow.

- The celebrant anoints the baby's breast with the oil of catechumens for protection from evil and for strengthening in Christ.

- All process to the font.

The Rite of Baptism
At the Font and After

✧ At the font the celebrant blesses the water. In this blessing we recall God's mighty deeds, God's grace, and the power of Baptism in the life of the Church.

✧ The parents and godparents together renounce sin and profess faith together on behalf of the child. The assembly gives its assent to this profession in spoken word or song.

✧ In the saving waters of the font, your godchild is baptized "in the name of the Father, and of the Son, and of the Holy Spirit." Your godchild is immersed three times or has water poured upon him or her three times.

✧ The celebrant anoints the crown of your godchild's head with chrism.

✧ You or the parents dress this child in the baptismal garment, which is an outward sign of Christian dignity.

- One of the godparents lights the godchild's candle from the Easter candle after the celebrant says, "Receive the light of Christ."

- A prayer for the opening of the ears and mouth to hear Christ's word and proclaim his faith may be prayed, at the discretion of the minister.

- Mass now continues in the usual way. If Baptism is celebrated outside Mass, everyone processes to the altar and prays the Lord's Prayer, and the liturgy concludes with a special blessing and dismissal.

Beyond Baptism
The Role of a Godparent

Where do you go from here? That will be up to you. Standing near the parents while the Baptism takes place is only the beginning of a lifelong relationship.

There is much more. Clearly this sacrament marks the beginning of a lasting relationship of your godchild with God and with the Church. The relationship of a godparent and a godchild grows and continues beyond the day of Baptism too.

Now is the time to begin. Start by praying for your godchild. Spend time with him or her when you can—especially as the years pass. Send notes, cards, e-mail messages. Phone from time to time. Take your godchild to Mass with you, pray together, and read the Bible together.

How will you mark the special days ahead? Birthdays and Christmas are obvious occasions for celebration, but what about celebrating the anniversary of Baptism? It will be easiest to give presents for different occasions, but consider how much more valuable your presence could be when your godchild needs someone to listen, to care, to teach, to advise.

How do you plan to assist and guide your godchild in the years to come?

Acknowledgments *(continued from page ii)*

Text

Scripture excerpts are taken from the *New American Bible with Revised New Testament and Psalms* copyright © 1991, 1986, 1970 Confraternity of Christian Doctrine, Inc., Washington D.C. Used with permission. All rights reserved. No part of the *New American Bible* may be reproduced by any means without permission in writing from the copyright owner.

Excerpts from *Catechism of the Catholic Church*. English translation of the *Catechism of the Catholic Church* for the United States of America copyright © 1994, United States Catholic Conference, Inc.—Libreria Editrice Vaticana.

Photographs

Photo page positions: top (t), middle (m), bottom (b), right (r), left (l)
Cover: Phil Martin Photography
Phil Martin Photography **ii, iii, 5, 8, 9, 11, 12, 13.** Getty images: Luc Beziat **6**, Barbara Peacock **7(tm)**, Harry Sieplinga/HMS Images **7(tr)**, Charles Thatcher **7(br)**, Jim Cummins **7(bl)**, Dag Sundberg **7(tl)**, China Tourism Press **16**, Yellow Dog Productions **17**. The Crosiers/Gene Plaisted OSC **10**. Diane Eichhold **15**. All other photographs from Loyola Press.